YOUNG MASTERS
Heart Of A Lion

Written by Bunny Hull

Illustrations by Kye Fleming

Edited by Wendy Werris

Layout & Typography by James Suelflow

ISBN 978-0-9826278-0-8

Little Wisdom Series
© 2010 Dream A World®

www.dreamaworld.com

Once upon a time, somewhere over the sky and under the moon, Butaan, Phylos and EEtha set foot on planet Earth for the very first time. Until then they had only heard stories about the powerful gifts born to the people of Earth.

Now they would learn all about them. What were the gifts? How were they used? It was there in a magic garden that their adventures began, as they sat by the stream and talked about the very important things they learned from Saphinne – *the secrets of the heart.*

"What do you say we cross over to the other side of the stream today?" asked EEtha.

"We can get there if we just step on the rocks — one, two, three, four... that's easy," said Butaan.

3

"I think it looks hard," said Phylos, "and why do we need to cross anyway?"

"Don't you want to see what the magic garden looks like over there?" asked EEtha.

"What if I lose my balance and fall in the water?" asked Phylos.

"What if you don't?" asked Butaan.

"But I've never done it before," said Phylos, "and I can't swim!"

"You can do it," said EEtha,

"besides the water is only up to our ankles.

Oh, look – Jolly is even giving Squeek a ride across."

"Do you think the people of Earth are ever afraid to try new things?" Phylos asked.

"Saphinne says they're really good at it," said Butaan.

"Good at what?" asked EEtha.

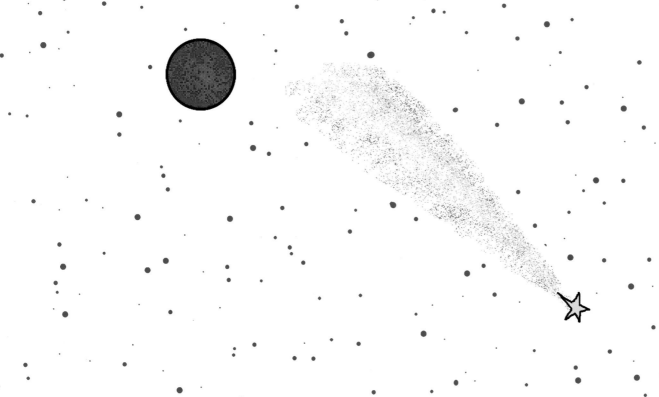

"Believing," said Butaan.

"Believing what?" asked Phylos.

"Well, Saphinne says you either believe you can
or you believe you can't," said Butaan.

"Can or can't what?" asked EEtha.

"Do something
mostly,"
said Butaan.

"What happens when you believe you can?" asked EEtha.

"That's called believing in yourself."

"And when you believe in yourself, your heart fills up with courage," said Butaan.

"What's courage?" asked EEtha.

"Saphinne says courage is something that melts your fears away
like they were snowflakes in the hot sun," said Butaan.

"Courage makes you feel brave."

"I'll bet when that happens you feel like you can do things you never thought you could do," said EEtha.

"When you're brave," said Phylos,

"you're not afraid of being alone..."

"Or being in the dark."

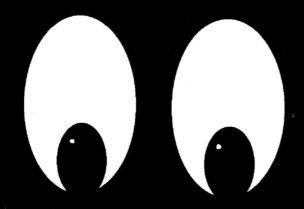

"When you're brave you have the heart of a lion," said Butaan, "fearless and strong."

"You know you're perfect just the way you are."

"Courage is not being afraid to tell someone how you feel," said EEtha.

"Courage is believing in things some people can't see," said Butaan.

"Courage makes you brave enough to walk away from a big bully," said Phylos, "or tell him to stop hitting you."

"Or brave enough to say no when someone asks you to do something you know isn't right," said Butaan.

"Oh, so having courage means being smart," said EEtha.

"A courageous heart is very smart," said Butaan.

"Are all the people of Earth born with courage?" asked Phylos.

"Saphinne says everyone has courage if they just believe,"
said Butaan. "It's a secret of the heart."

"Courage is believing you can go anywhere and make a new friend."

"I believe in myself," said EEtha. "I am EEtha the great!"

"Courage is knowing you can learn anything."

"I believe in myself," said Butaan. "I am Butaan the brilliant!"

"Courage is knowing you can do anything."

"I believe in myself," roared Phylos. "I am Phylos the brave. I have the heart of a lion. Onward…let us cross the stream!"

Who are you and how did you show your courage today?

Thank you for being here!

Download the song lyrics and activity pages at www.dreamaworld.com

"The Young Masters Pledge," "Here We Go," "Heart of A Lion – Story,"
"Roar Like A Lion," "The Heart Is Very Smart," "I Am Courage," "Hey Young Master,"
"What Can I Learn Today," "Thank You For Being Here," "Asanti Ku kuwa Hapa" (Swahili),
All songs produced, written and performed by Bunny Hull

"Asanti Ku kuwa Hapa" - Swahili Translation by Anindo Marshall

"Young Masters Pledge" and "Heart of A Lion – Story" are narrated by by Elayn J. Taylor

Flute: Diane Hsu * Guitar: James Harrah
Harmonica: Peter "Madcat" Ruth * Ukulele: Steve Rose
Percussion and Additional vocals: Anindo Marshall
Children's background vocals: Jadah Fahnbulleh & Saamera Jamai
Additional percussion: Jeff Hull * Multimedia voiceovers: Lauren Wood

Recorded by Bunny Hull
Mixed by Jeff Hull at Dream A World Studios
Mastering: Dwarf Village Studios, Valley Village

Dedicated to my father, my teachers and the many friends who share and
support my vision for children everywhere…especially Char and IPA.

ISBN 978-0-9826278-0-8

Little Wisdom Series
© 2010 Dream A World®

www.dreamaworld.com

Bunny Hull – Author, Songwriter

A resident of Los Angeles, California, Hull is a Grammy Award®-winning songwriter and recipient of over 20 Gold and Platinum albums, with songs that have appeared on television and in films which include *The Prince Of Egypt*, *Bruce Almighty*, *Sesame Street*, *Oprah*, *The Simpsons* and *Evan Almighty*.

In the world of children's books and music, Hull is the recipient of a Parents' Choice Award, Three National Parenting Publication Awards, two Dr. Toy Awards and a Parent's Guide To Children's Media Award. Hull's non-profit, Dream A World Education, Inc. currently serves children in the Los Angeles area, using music and the arts to empower children 4–7 to learn about self-image, diversity, relationships and the universal principles that join us as a global family.

Kye Fleming – Illustrator

A Nashville, Tennessee resident, Fleming comes from the music world where she has established a career as an award-winning songwriter; three time BMI Writer of the Year; and Grammy, CMA, ACM and Dove nominee. Other awards include Billboard Song of the Year and in 2009 she was inducted into the Nashville Songwriter Association International Songwriters Hall of Fame.

Art is something that comes naturally, and her computerized characters emerged when Fleming purchased an iBook a few years ago. These drawings are created with AppleWorks, a finger and a track pad. "Young Masters" is Fleming's entry into the world of illustration. Personal philosophies: Motivation: fun; Inspiration: life; Perspiration: I don't believe in it; Advice: pet your cat.

Elayn J. Taylor – Saphinne, Our Storyteller

Elayn lives in Los Angeles and has appeared in film and on television including, *Bruce Almighty*, *Something's Gotta Give*, *Rules of Engagement*, *Dr. Doolittle 2*, *Sabrina*, *Strong Medicine*, *The Practice*, *True Blood* and more. Her stage appearances include *Rose in Fences*, *Gem Of The Ocean* (L.A.), *Someplace Soft To Fall* (St. Paul), and *Joe Turner* (Houston).

Diane Hsu – Flute

Diane lives in Los Angeles and performed as a concerto soloist from the age of 11 with the Seattle Philharmonic Orchestra, the Northwest Chamber Orchestra, the University of Washington Symphony and has been a selected participant in Boston University's Tanglewood Institute. Also an actress, she has appeared on film and in television in *How Stella Got Her Groove Back, Snapdragon, Totally Blonde, James Bond: License To Kill, The West Wing, Family Matters, Sunset Beach, Bloodlines* and more.

Anindo Marshall – Percussion and Vocals

Anindo began her musical and dance career in her homeland of Kenya as a vocalist, dancer and percussionist. She enjoyed a successful solo career in Europe as a vocalist, signing a recording contract with EMI Spain, and becoming known as Kenya's singing sensation. Anindo was musical and technical advisor on *Survivor Africa*, has worked on films *Kazaam, Congo* and *Ali,* and has performed with Babatunde Olatunji, and Mickey Hart of the Grateful Dead, among others. She is a certified Dunham Technique instructor and member of all female vocal group called AADAWE.

Also available from Dream A World

The Friendship Seed	*Peace In Our Land*
The Magic Eye	*Dream A World*
The Hidden Treasure	*Alphabet Affirmations*
Secrets of the Heart	*Creative World*
The Invisible Power	*A Child's Spirit*
This Little Light	*Happy Happy Kwanzaa*

www.dreamaworld.com